Tiny Travellers
in
LONDON

By Carol Moreira
Illustrated by Reiko Sakaguchi

ISBN 1 901334 01 5

The publisher wishes to thank the following for their assistance in writing and researching this book: The Apollo Victoria Theatre, Hamleys, Harrods, Madame Tussaud's, The Really Useful Company, and St Martin's Theatre.

A great writer once said that when someone is tired of London they are tired of life. The writer, Samuel Johnson, meant that London is so exciting that it's like life itself – good fun with lots of opportunities for learning. London has palaces, ancient towers, museums, parks, theatres and much more.

If you hear someone talk about "The City", they're talking abou business district, known for its men in pin-striped suits.

St. George, England's national saint, was a Roman officer who spoke out against the killing of Christians. He is usually shown fighting a dragon, which represents his battle against this evil practice.

London has 7 million residents. It is the capital of the United Kingdom, which means England, Scotland, Wales and Northern Ireland. It is the home of both the Prime Minister, who heads the government, and the Queen, who is the symbolic head of state. It is also a centre for sports, the arts and business.

The famous Tower Bridge was opened in 1894. It is the most beautiful bridge across the Thames, which is the river that winds through London.

There are about 3,000 red phone boxes in central London.

L ondon is a jolly old city. People rush to work on the tube, as the underground train system is called, and they work hard. But after work they enjoy themselves at the theatre or at concerts or near the flashing neon lights of Piccadilly Circus. It's fun to roll around on a red double–decker bus, or in a big black taxi and see how people live. Some live in big old homes joined together in a row. These homes are more than 100 years old and date from the time of Queen Victoria. They are called terraces.

Did you know London taxi drivers have to pass stiff exams before they can drive a cab? Sometimes they spend years studying for their exams.

British Police are sometimes called Bobbies, named after Sir Robert Peel, who formed the police force in 1829.

Londoners can choose between many different daily newspapers. The main television station, the BBC, is one of the best in the world. Two favourite dishes are sausages and mashed potatoes (known as bangers and mash) and fish and chips. There are restaurants from many cultures, because London is home to people from all over the world. Some come from countries that used to be part of the British Empire.

...ube" has 18 different lines, ranging from the old, rattling ...rn Line, built in the 19th Century, to the new Jubilee Line.

Buckingham Palace is the home of Queen Elizabeth the Second, the Queen of Great Britain and the British Commonwealth. Each morning at 11:30, the soldiers who guard the Queen perform a colourful ceremony called the Changing of the Guard.

The soldiers at Buckingham Palace wear red coats and big, furry black hats called buzbies. The hats are made from Canadian bearskins. You can go inside the Palace in August and September.

All kings and queens since William the Conqueror have been crowned in Westminster Abbey. It is also the place where royals get married, except for Prince Charles and Lady Diana Spencer who were married at St Paul's Cathedral in 1981. Many famous people, including Queen Elizabeth the First and the English writer Charles Dickens, are buried here too. Look for Dickens' picture on a ten-pound note.

said Queen Elizabeth the First r had a husband because she was ied to England.

Guess the last time England was invaded. It was 1066, when William the Conqueror sailed from France and defeated English troops at Hastings.

King Henry was famous for having six wives. Visit his castle at Windsor, near London. The castle was originally built by William the Conqueror.

King Henry the Eighth used to hunt in Hyde Park almost 500 years ago. Today, it's just one of the many great places in London for a picnic. Hampstead Heath is so peaceful it's hard to believe you are in London. At Greenwich Park, you can ramble through the wooded park. At the water-front, look around the 19th century ship, *The Cutty Sark*, which used to bring tea from China.

It is traditional to enjo bowl of strawberries a cream at Wimbledon.

Not far from London, the universities of Oxford and Cambridge hold their annual rowing races.

Tennis anyone? The world's most famous tennis tournament – Wimbledon – is held each summer and features the best men and women players in the world. You can also visit the Wimbledon Museum. Wimbledon is only one of London's sports attractions. You can also join the singing fans at a football match or rugby game. Relax in the sun at a cricket match, but don't try to watch the whole match – they last for days.

The Houses of Parliament, known as the Palace of Westminster, are the centre of Britain's Government. Parliament opened in 1265. The buildings, which you can visit, include the House of Lords and the House of Commons.

The prime minister lives at 10 Downing Street. You will often see him on television meeting people at his door.

Britain's Parliament is famous around the world for the huge chiming clock known as Big Ben.

A statue of Winston Churchill, who was Prime Minister during the Second World War, stands outside the Parliament buildings.

The first St. Paul's Cathedral was destroyed by the Great Fire of London in 1666. The new St. Paul's was built to replace it and was designed by the great architect, Sir Christopher Wren. Wren is buried in the cathedral, along with the Duke of Wellington, who defeated Napoleon in battle in 1815.

In 1605, a group of Catholics, including Guy Fawkes, tried to blow up King James in Parliament. Each November 5th, bonfires are lit and fireworks are set off across Britain to celebrate Guy Fawkes Day.

n Victoria was on the throne for ars and ruled over an empire overed one quarter of the Earth.

The Tower of London was once a prison for enemies of the Royal Family. Parts of it still have eerie names like the Bloody Tower and Traitors' Gate. Today you can see where these prisoners were held, where they died and where they were buried. There are also rooms filled with suits of armour worn by the kings of England.

There are usually six ravens at the Tower of London. Legend says that if the ravens leave, the tower and the kingdom will fall. Can you count all six?

The Tower is the home of the Crown Jewels, which are worn by the Royal Family on important occasions.

he National Gallery stands at the top of Trafalgar
Square. Britain's most important art gallery has
,200 paintings from the last seven centuries.

Trafalgar Square contains fountains where visitors love to relax and have their photo taken with the pigeons who flock there. The square is named after the Battle of Trafalgar, in which Britain's Lord Nelson defeated the French navy in 1805. There is a huge monument to Nelson. There are also bronze lions, said to be made from cannon captured from the French.

nen, sometimes called
eaters, used to guard the
er. Today they are tour guides.

Can you name these famous people you can see at Madame Tussaud's?

Want your picture taken with a movie star or a king? Head to Madame Tussaud's, London's wax museum. Next door, explore the universe in a Space Trail voyage at the London Planetarium.

See a real space ship at the National Museum of Science. The basement is like an indoor playground packed with scientific toys.

In the Victoria and Albert Museum, you can see relics from around the world. See dinosaurs and prehistoric animals at the Museum of Natural History.

The Spirit of London tour at Madame Tussaud's takes you through 400 years of London's history in a black taxi.

The British Library has 10 million books, stacked on 110 miles of shelves.

The British Museum, which opened in 1753, displays the work of people from prehistoric times to today. There are mummies of ancient Egyptian kings and queens and Greek statues more than 2,000 years old. There is also a Roman Britain exhibition where you can learn about these ancient invaders.

Exhibitions of old cultures and exotic civilizations are held at the British Museum. One of the most famous was the display about the Egyptian king Tutankhamen.

Londod's theatres are advertised everywhere including on the Tube and on buses. London is famous all over the world for its excellent plays, and has been for a long time. The world's greatest playwright, William Shakespeare, lived in London 400 years ago and wrote such plays as Hamlet and Macbeth. His theatre, the Globe, is being rebuilt using the same materials as they used in the original. It's open for you to visit.

In Cats, a play based on poems by T.S. Eliot, all th actors are dressed like cats. Britain has produced of the biggest rock stars ever. There's even a Rock roll museum in Piccadilly Circus.

You can enjoy modern plays, such as Starlight Express, where the actors are dressed like trains and wear roller skates. Or, if you visit around Christmas, you might like a pantomime.

It's a silly sort of English play where the main female character is played by a man and the main male is played by a woman. The Mousetrap, by Agatha Christie, has been shown almost every day for more than 40 years. Some of the best shows in London, including concerts and operas, are at the Royal Albert Hall.

Sherlock Holmes, with his pipe and hat, is London's most famous story-book detective. There's a store dedicated to him on Baker Street, where he was said to live.

SHERLOCK HOLMES
CONSULTING DETECTIVE
22th Baker Street

Harrod's

London has always been a place where people come for shopping. Some streets are even named after the things once sold there. Poultry is the name of one street where they used to sell chickens. Oxford and Regent streets give you a feeling of what London was like 100 years ago. Although they have very modern shops, they have lots of beautiful old buildings.

Take a break from shopping and enjoy scor and tea. Scones are hard buns with raisins average Briton drinks five cups of tea every

Petticoat Lane is a huge Sunday morning market that got its name in the 17th century when clothes sellers worked there.

Harrods is London's most famous department store. At night it is lit up by 11,500 lights. It has a huge toy department. If you like toys, you will love Hamleys, one of the world's best toy stores.

In Covent Garden, you can watch a juggler or pause for a bite to eat. Camden Lock Market is open every weekend on the water at Regent's Canal.

Want to sit in a train that ran over 100 years ago? You can at the Transport Museum in Covent Garden.

W ant to have breakfast with a barracuda and lunch with a leopard? Then head to Regent's Park to see the London Zoo and the London Aquarium. The zoo has all sorts of animals, from aardvarks to zebras. There's a Moonlight World, which is kept dark so we can see how animals act at night. The Aquarium has tanks filled with weird and exciting fish, like stingrays and octopuses.

Dick Whittington was a poor 13th century boy who became rich after he sold his cat to a foreign king to kill rats and mice. Dick eventually became Lord Mayor of London three times.

If you love ships, visit the National Maritime Museum in Greenwich where you can learn all about Britain's historic navy. On top of the nearby hill, is the Old Royal Observatory, where generations of great scientists have studied the stars. It was founded by King Charles the Second in 1675 and designed by Christopher Wren. You can look at old telescopes and clocks and stand astride the Meridian Line, the basis for all the world's time zones.

PARENTS' GUIDE TO LONDON

This book has been designed to expose children to interesting, educational and fun aspects of London. Following is a description of the attractions with the price (as of November 1996), address, nearest tube station, telephone number and opening hours.

Key: All prices are in Sterling (1 pound equalled roughly US$1.63 at the time of printing).

CLIMATE:

London has a moderate climate, and its reputation for fog and rain is vastly exaggerated. The summers are pleasantly mild, although children will probably need sweaters for the evenings. The winters are wet and cold enough to warrant boots and heavy coats, but there is rarely sufficient snow to form drifts.

SAFETY TIPS:

Although London has lower crime rates than major U.S. cities, parents should still keep a close eye on children at all times. Tap water is safe for drinking; bottled water is also widely available. Fruits and vegetables should be washed. Foreigners should be careful crossing the street, as cars in the near lane will approach from the right. At the time of printing this book, the Irish Republican Army had not reinstated its ceasefire. Although acts of terrorism are rare, people should avoid and report unattended bags in streets or on the Underground.

1. Regent's Park
2. Hyde Park
3. Science Museum
4. Natural History Museum
5. Victoria & Albert Museum
6. Buckingham Palace
7. St James's Park
8. Westminster Abbey
9. Houses of Parliament
10. National Gallery
11. British Museum
12. St Paul's Cathedral

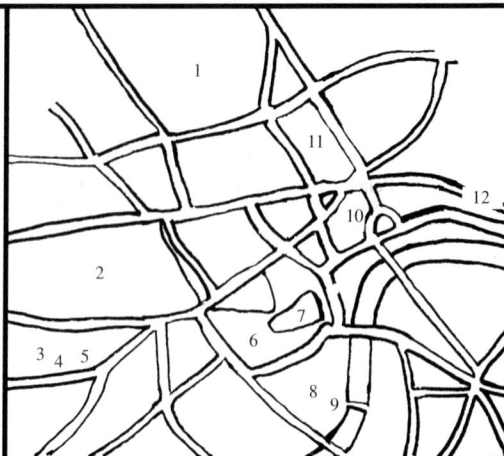

TELEPHONE NUMBERS:

Emergencies (Police, Fire, Ambulances) 999
London Tourist Board Visitor Call: 0839 123 456
Parents and children tourist information: 0839 123 424
London Tourist Board Information Centre: 0891 505 470 (bus and walking tours)
Travel Information Centres: 0171 222 1234
London Tourist Board River Trips: 0839 1234 32
London Tourist Board Special Events: 0839 123 404
Kidsline 0171 222 8070 (Information on children's activities and entertainment)

Missing Persons Freecall 0500 700700
Theatre Information – Ticket Line 0171 396 4738
Lost property:
British Rail 0171 928 5151
London Transport 0171 486 2496
or write London Transport at: Lost Property, 200 Baker St., W1, Open 9:30 am-2 pm Mon-Fri.

ATTRACTIONS:

TOWER BRIDGE (Pages 2 & 3): Tower Bridge Museum tells of the bridge's history and engineering achievement. Tower Hill tube station. Tel: 0171 407 0922. Museum open: 10 am-6:30 pm Apr-Oct; 9:30-6 Nov-Mar. Entry to museum: £5.50, children £3.75, under fives free.

BUCKINGHAM PALACE (Pages 6 & 7): Get to the palace before 11 am for assembly of guards in the courtyard at 11:30. Guards change every day in summer and once every two days in winter (August-Easter). St. James Park tube station. Tel: 0171 930 4832. Buckingham Palace tours: Aug-Sept only. Tickets: £9.00, children under 17 £5.00.

WESTMINSTER ABBEY (Pages 6 & 7): Westminster or St. James Park tube station. Open: 9 am-2:45 pm Mon-Fri, 9-2:45 and 3:45-5 Sat. Closed Sun. Tel: 0171 222 5152. Entry: £4, children under 16 £1.

CUTTY SARK (Pages 8 & 9): King William Walk, Greenwich Pier. Go to Island Gardens station on the Docklands Light Railway and take the tunnel under the Thames, or go to British Rail at Greenwich, or take buses 177, 180, 188, 199, 286 or 386. Open: Jun-Sep 10 am-6 pm, Mon-Sat, 12-6 Sun; Oct-May 10 am-5 pm Mon-Sat. Tel: 0181-858 3445. Entry: £3.50, children £2.50, families (2 adults and up to 3 children) £8.50, under fives free.

WIMBLEDON (Pages 8 & 9): All England Lawn Tennis and Croquet Club, Church Road, Wimbledon. Tel: 0181 946 2244. Wimbledon Fortnight is during the last week of June and the first week of July. Wimbledon tube or British Rail. Tennis museum: History of tennis, video theatre, stand on a viewing platform above centre court.

Tel: 0181 944 1066. Open: Tues-Sat 10:30 am-5 pm, Sun 2-5, closed Mon. £2.50 adults, £1.50 children.

WINDSOR CASTLE (Pages 8 & 9): Visit at 11 am for the Changing of the Guard – alternate days in winter. Attractions include Queen Mary's Dolls House. Opening hours depend on whether the Royal Family is present. Check with Castle Information Office. Tel: 01753 831 118. Cost: £8.50, under 17 £4.50, family £19.50 (2 adults and 2 children), when all the rooms are open, plus £1.00 extra to see Queen Mary's Dolls House.

HOUSES OF PARLIAMENT (Pages 10 &11): St. Margaret St. SW1. Tel: 0171-219-3000. Westminster tube station. Entrance to the House of Commons during debates by application to your MP (or embassy for foreigners) or by queuing. Tours of Westminster Hall and the Palace of Westminster by application to MP or for overseas visitors, by writing to the Public Information Office at 1 Derby Gate, Westminster, London, SW1A 2DG. No charge for tours, guides can be arranged through the office for about £20.

ST. PAUL'S CATHEDRAL (Pages 10 & 11): St Paul's tube station. Open: 8:30 am-4 pm Mon-Sat, except during special services. Tel: 0171 246 8320. Entry: £6, children 6-16, £3, includes entrance to the galleries.

TOWER OF LONDON (Pages 12 & 13): Tower Hill tube station. Open: 9 am-5 pm, Tues-Sat, 10-5 Sun and Mon. Tel: 0171-709-0765. Entry: £8.30, children aged 5-15 £5.50, family ticket (not more than two adults) £21.95.

NATIONAL GALLERY (Pages 12 & 13): Trafalgar Square, Charing Cross, Leicester Square or Piccadilly Circus tubes. Open: 10 am-6 pm, Mon-Sat, and until 8 pm Wed, noon-6 Sun. Tel: 0171 747 2885. No charge.

MADAME TUSSAUD'S AND THE LONDON PLANETARIUM (Pages 14 & 15): Marylebone Rd. NW1. Baker Street tube station. Tel: 0171 935 6861. Open 10 am-5:30 pm weekdays, 9:30-5:30 weekends. Tickets: combined with the London Planetarium £10.95, under 16 £6.95; for Madame Tussaud's only £8.75, under 16 £5.75; Planetarium only, £5.45, children £3.60. Planetarium shows play every 40 minutes.

NATIONAL MUSEUM OF SCIENCE AND INDUSTRY (Pages 14 & 15): Exhibition Rd., SW7. Next to the Victoria and Albert Museum. South Kensington tube station. Tel: 0171 938 8080. Open: 10 am-6 pm Mon-Sun. Entry: £5.50, 5-17 year olds £2.90, under fives free.

BRITISH MUSEUM (Pages 14 & 15): Great Russell St, WC1. Tottenham Court Road tube station. The museum currently includes the British Library, although the library is in the process of moving to 96 Euston Road. The move will be completed by 1999. Open: 10 am-5 pm, Mon-Sat, 2.30-6 Sun. Films, lectures, Tue-Sat. Tel: 0171 636 1555. Free (charge for special exhibitions and guided tours).

VICTORIA AND ALBERT MUSEUM (Pages 14 & 15): Cromwell Rd SW7. South Kensington tube station. Open: 10 am-5:50 pm Tue-Sun, 12-5:50 Mon. Tel: 0171 938 8500. Entry: £5, children free.

THE NATURAL HISTORY MUSEUM (Pages 14 & 15): Cromwell Rd, SW7 5BD. South Kensington tube. 10 am-6 pm Mon-Sat, 11-6 Sun. Tel: 0171 938 9123. Entry: £5.50, ages 5-17 £2.80, family £15.

SHAKESPEARE GLOBE MUSEUM (Pages 16 & 17): 1 Bear Gardens, Bankside, SE1. London Bridge or Mansion House tube. Shakespeare's Globe Exhibition tells the story of the reconstruction of Shakespeare's Globe Theatre, using the traditional materials and building techniques of 400 years ago. Entrance to the exhibition includes a guided tour of the theatre. Open: 10 am-5 pm, including all bank holidays. Closed 24 and 25 December. Tel: 0171-928-6406. Entry: £5, children £3, families (two adults and two children) £14.

ROYAL ALBERT HALL (Pages 16 & 17): Kensington Gore, SW7. South Kensington tube station. 0171 589 8212. Prices and times vary.

THE MOUSETRAP (Pages 16 & 17): Playing at St Martin's Theatre, West Street, WC2. Leicester Square tube station. 0171 836 1443. Each evening at 8 pm. Matinees at 2:45 Tues and 5 pm Sat. Tickets from £9 in the week, £11 Fri or Sat.

STARLIGHT EXPRESS (Pages 16 & 17): Playing at the Apollo Victoria Theatre. Wilton Road, SW1. Victoria Tube Station. Tel 0171 416 6045. Play begins at 7:45 pm Mon-Sat. Matinees at 3 pm Tues and Sat. Tickets from £12.50.

CATS (Pages 16 & 17): New London Theatre, Drury Lane. Holborn or Covent Garden tube stations. Tel: 0171 405 0072. Mon-Sat show starts at 7:45 pm. Tickets from £10.50. Matinee: 3 pm Tues and Sat.

MADAME TUSSAUD'S ROCK CIRCUS (Pages 16 & 17): London Pavilion, Piccadilly, W1. Tel: 0171 734 8025. Madame Tussaud's waxworks and audio animatronic techniques make the rock stars look and sound lifelike. Open 11 am-9 pm Mon, Wed, Thur & Sun, 12.00-9 Tue, 12.00-10.00 pm Fri and Sat. Entry: £7.50, under 16 £5.95, family (two adults and two children) £19.95.

HAMLEYS (Pages 18 & 19): 188-196 Regent Street. Oxford Circus tube station. Open 10 am-7 pm six days a week, 6 pm Sun. Tel: 0171 734 3161.

HARRODS (Pages 18 & 19):

Knightsbridge SW1. Knightsbridge tube station. Tel: 0171 730 1234. Open: 10 am-6 pm Mon, Tues and Sat, 10-7 Wed-Fri.

TRANSPORT MUSEUM (Pages 18 & 19): Covent Garden. Covent Garden tube station. 10 am-6 pm six days a week, 11-6 Fri. Tel: 0171 379 6344. Charge: Entry £4.50, ages 5-15 £2.50.

LONDON ZOO AND AQUARIUM (Pages 20 & 21): Regent's Park, NW1. Camden Town tube station. The number 274 bus leaves Camden Town and Baker Street for the zoo. Open: Mar-Oct 10 am-5:30 pm, Mon-Sun; Nov-Feb, 10-dusk, Mon-Sun. Tel: 0171 722 3333. Entry charge (includes entry to Aquarium): £7.80, ages 4-14 £5.70, family (two adults and two children or one adult, three children) £22.

NATIONAL MARITIME MUSEUM and OLD ROYAL OBSERVATORY: (Pages 20 & 21): Romney Rd., SE10. (Same directions as The Cutty Sark, Pages 7 & 8) Open: 10 am-5 pm seven days a week. Closed Dec 24-26. Tel: 0181 858 4422. Entry charge (includes museum and observatory): £5.50, children £3, under fives free.

THE ROYAL BOTANIC GARDENS AT KEW (Pages 20 & 21): Kew Gardens tube station. Open 9:30 am-4 pm every day except Christmas and New Year's. Entry: £4.50, ages 5-16 £2.50, family £12. Tel: 0181 940 1171.